PRINCEWILL LAGANG

Riding High: The Untold Story of Alice Walton and the Rise of Walmart's Fortune

First published by PRINCEWILL LAGANG 2023

Copyright © 2023 by Princewill Lagang

All rights reserved. No part of this publication may be reproduced, stored or transmitted in any form or by any means, electronic, mechanical, photocopying, recording, scanning, or otherwise without written permission from the publisher. It is illegal to copy this book, post it to a website, or distribute it by any other means without permission.

Princewill Lagang asserts the moral right to be identified as the author of this work.

First edition

This book was professionally typeset on Reedsy.
Find out more at reedsy.com

Contents

1 Introduction — 1
2 A Legacy in the Ozarks — 3
3 The Walmart Revolution — 5
4 A Visionary's Dilemma — 7
5 The Art of Reinvention — 9
6 The Legacy Unfolds — 11
7 Reflections and Continuity — 13
8 A New Horizon — 15
9 The Ever-Expanding Ripple — 17
10 Beyond Fortune: Lessons from the Walmart Legacy — 19
11 Legacy in Motion: Navigating the Future — 21
12 The Unfinished Canvas: Charting New Horizons — 23
13 Embracing the Unpredictable: Walmart's Odyssey — 25
14 Summary — 28

1

Introduction

"Riding High: The Untold Story of Alice Walton and the Rise of Walmart's Fortune" unfolds as an illuminating narrative that traverses the dynamic landscape of retail, business acumen, and the indomitable spirit of a family that shaped one of the world's most influential corporations. At the heart of this narrative is Alice Walton, a formidable force in the Walmart saga and a key figure in the Walton family's legacy.

This chronicle begins in the scenic Ozark Mountains, where Alice Walton's journey unfolds against the backdrop of her family's modest beginnings. As the youngest child of Sam and Helen Walton, Alice was witness to the early entrepreneurial ventures that laid the groundwork for what would become the global retail giant, Walmart.

The narrative is a tapestry woven through decades, each chapter a vibrant thread that brings to life the pivotal moments in the evolution of Walmart. From the revolutionary Walmart Discount City store in the 1960s to the digital transformation of the 21st century, the story encapsulates the resilience, innovation, and strategic vision that propelled Walmart to unprecedented heights.

As Alice Walton rises through the ranks, the narrative delves into her unique role in shaping Walmart's destiny. Her leadership during times of technological disruption, commitment to social responsibility, and influence on the corporate culture form the crux of this untold story.

The Walton family's legacy is not confined to boardrooms and balance sheets; it extends to philanthropy, community engagement, and a commitment to sustainable business practices. This narrative explores how the Walton Family Foundation became a vessel for impactful initiatives, leaving an enduring mark on education, environmental conservation, and healthcare.

"Riding High" seeks to unravel the intricacies of a family-founded empire, offering a nuanced portrayal of Alice Walton's leadership and the multifaceted evolution of Walmart. As the chapters unfold, readers are invited to traverse the aisles of history, witnessing the triumphs, challenges, and ongoing legacy of a corporation that has become synonymous with the global retail landscape. In each turn of the page, the narrative endeavors to unveil the untold facets of Alice Walton's journey and the remarkable ascent of Walmart's fortune.

2

A Legacy in the Ozarks

The sun dipped below the horizon, casting long shadows over the rolling hills of the Ozark Mountains. In the quiet town of Newport, Arkansas, a small clapboard house nestled amidst the trees bore witness to the birth of a legacy that would echo through the corridors of commerce for generations to come.

Alice Walton came into the world on October 7, 1949, the youngest of four children born to Helen and Sam Walton. Even in those early days, the air in the Ozarks carried the scent of opportunity. Sam, a tenacious and visionary entrepreneur, had already tried his hand at several ventures, laying the groundwork for the empire that would later become Walmart.

The family lived modestly, but the seeds of ambition were sown early in Alice's life. As a child, she often accompanied her father on buying trips, absorbing the principles of retail that would become the cornerstone of her future success. Sam's stores, a string of Ben Franklin franchises, were the testing grounds where Alice first glimpsed the dynamics of customer service, supply chain management, and the art of the deal.

The Walton household buzzed with an entrepreneurial spirit that transcended their humble surroundings. Alice, even as a young girl, exhibited a keen interest in the family business. Her afternoons were spent poring over store ledgers, and she could often be found rearranging shelves, an innate sense of order and aesthetics guiding her young hands.

But the road to retail royalty was not without its challenges. The Waltons weathered financial storms and navigated the unpredictable terrain of the retail landscape. Through it all, Alice observed, absorbed, and quietly developed her own understanding of the industry's ebbs and flows.

As the 1960s dawned, so did a new era for the Waltons. Sam, ever the innovator, opened the first Walmart Discount City store in Rogers, Arkansas, in 1962. The concept was revolutionary—a one-stop-shop offering a wide array of goods at discounted prices. The retail landscape would never be the same.

For Alice, this marked the beginning of a journey that would see her rise from the shadows of her family's success to carve out her own niche in the business world. The Walton children were no strangers to hard work, and Alice, driven by a potent mix of filial duty and personal ambition, dove headfirst into the world of retail.

Chapter 1 sets the stage for the saga of Alice Walton and the rise of Walmart's fortune. Against the backdrop of the Ozarks, the reader is introduced to the formative years of the Walton family and the early days of Walmart—a retail revolution in the making. As Alice grows up amidst the hustle and bustle of her father's stores, the foundations are laid for her eventual ascent in the business world. The stage is set for a tale of ambition, innovation, and the inexorable march of Walmart towards becoming a global retail giant.

3

The Walmart Revolution

The 1970s unfolded with a sense of anticipation in the air as Walmart embarked on an expansion spree, opening stores across the heartland of America. Alice Walton, a young and dynamic force within the company, found herself at the epicenter of this retail revolution. As the landscape of the retail industry shifted, so too did Alice's role within the Walmart empire.

The small-town discount store model proved to be a winning formula, and Walmart's footprint grew rapidly. Alice, armed with her father's teachings and her own insights, played a pivotal role in streamlining operations. Her keen eye for detail and a relentless pursuit of efficiency earned her the respect of her peers and colleagues.

As Walmart rose to prominence, so did the Walton family's wealth. The Waltons were no longer just business owners; they were a retail dynasty, and Alice, often overshadowed by her more publicly visible siblings, quietly honed her skills in the shadows. Behind the scenes, she became a key player in shaping Walmart's identity and culture.

Alice's influence extended beyond the boardroom. The 1980s saw her spearhead initiatives to enhance Walmart's community engagement and corporate responsibility. Her commitment to philanthropy and a dedication to supporting local economies set a precedent for the company's future endeavors.

However, the path to success was not without its obstacles. The 1990s brought challenges, including criticism of Walmart's business practices and labor policies. As controversies brewed, Alice faced the daunting task of navigating the company through turbulent waters while upholding the values instilled by her father.

Amidst the challenges, Alice's vision for Walmart evolved. She recognized the potential of technology and embraced the digital age. Under her leadership, Walmart became an early adopter of e-commerce, further solidifying its position as an industry leader.

Chapter 2 delves into the transformative era of the 1970s to the 1990s, exploring Alice Walton's role in shaping Walmart's expansion, culture, and response to societal changes. As Walmart emerged as a retail giant, Alice's journey unfolded against the backdrop of economic shifts, technological advancements, and societal expectations. The chapter paints a vivid portrait of a woman navigating the complexities of business, family legacy, and corporate responsibility, setting the stage for the subsequent chapters in the untold story of Alice Walton and the rise of Walmart's fortune.

4

A Visionary's Dilemma

The dawn of the new millennium brought with it a wave of change that rippled through the retail landscape. In the corridors of Walmart's headquarters, Alice Walton faced a pivotal moment, standing at the crossroads of tradition and innovation. The question lingered: How could one of the world's largest retailers adapt to an increasingly dynamic and digital market?

As the 2000s unfolded, Alice took the helm of Walmart's strategic direction. The rise of e-commerce presented both a challenge and an opportunity. The retail behemoth that had once conquered Main Street now grappled with the complexities of the virtual marketplace. Alice, however, saw beyond the challenges, envisioning a Walmart that seamlessly blended brick-and-mortar prowess with cutting-edge digital strategies.

Under her leadership, Walmart invested heavily in technology and logistics. The company underwent a digital transformation, embracing online retail and omnichannel strategies. Alice's foresight in recognizing the importance of e-commerce positioned Walmart as a formidable player in the rapidly evolving world of online retail.

Yet, the journey was not without its setbacks. The transition to e-commerce brought about internal restructuring, and Walmart faced scrutiny for its impact on smaller businesses and local economies. Alice, cognizant of the delicate balance between progress and responsibility, steered the company through a maze of public relations challenges.

Beyond the boardroom, Alice's commitment to philanthropy reached new heights. The Walton Family Foundation became a vehicle for impactful initiatives, addressing education, environmental sustainability, and healthcare. Alice's influence extended beyond the aisles of Walmart, leaving an indelible mark on communities and causes close to her heart.

As the decade unfolded, Alice's leadership style, often described as measured and deliberate, faced the ultimate test. The global financial crisis of 2008 sent shockwaves through the business world, prompting tough decisions and strategic recalibrations. Alice's ability to navigate Walmart through economic turbulence underscored her resilience and strategic acumen.

Chapter 3 explores the early 21st century, a period of profound transformation for Walmart under Alice Walton's leadership. The chapter delves into the challenges and triumphs of steering a retail giant through the digital age, examining the delicate balance between innovation, corporate responsibility, and the enduring legacy of the Walton family. As the narrative unfolds, readers witness Alice's visionary approach to leadership and the intricate dance between tradition and progress in the ever-evolving saga of Walmart's fortune.

5

The Art of Reinvention

As the second decade of the 21st century dawned, Alice Walton found herself at the helm of a Walmart that was both a retail juggernaut and a digital pioneer. The company's relentless pursuit of innovation under her leadership was transforming not only the way people shopped but also the very essence of retail itself.

The early 2010s marked a period of reinvention for Walmart, and Alice was determined to lead the charge. The retail landscape was evolving at an unprecedented pace, with new players entering the arena and consumer expectations reaching new heights. E-commerce was no longer an option but a necessity, and Alice, with her finger on the pulse of the industry, steered Walmart through a series of strategic initiatives.

Under her guidance, Walmart further expanded its online presence, embracing cutting-edge technologies such as artificial intelligence and data analytics. The company's commitment to a seamless shopping experience became evident through innovations like online grocery shopping, curbside pickup, and a renewed focus on sustainability.

Alice's vision extended beyond the digital realm. The Walmart of the 2010s became synonymous with inclusivity and diversity. Initiatives to empower women in the workforce and support minority-owned businesses reflected a commitment to social responsibility that went hand in hand with the company's commercial success.

However, the winds of change also brought challenges. Walmart faced increased competition not only from traditional rivals but also from disruptive startups. The delicate balance between maintaining Walmart's legacy as a family-founded enterprise and adapting to the demands of a rapidly evolving market required strategic finesse.

The international stage became another arena for Walmart's expansion, with Alice overseeing the company's forays into emerging markets. The global reach of the brand brought both opportunities and complexities, requiring a nuanced understanding of diverse cultures and economic landscapes.

As the chapter unfolds, readers witness Alice Walton's deft navigation of the intricate dance between tradition and innovation. The corporate giant that emerged from this era was not only a testament to Walmart's ability to adapt but also a reflection of Alice's leadership philosophy—one that blended the wisdom of the past with the dynamism of the future.

Chapter 4 captures the essence of a transformative period in Walmart's history, exploring the challenges and triumphs of reinvention in the face of a rapidly changing retail landscape. The narrative takes readers on a journey through the corridors of power, where strategic decisions and visionary leadership shape the destiny of one of the world's most influential corporations.

6

The Legacy Unfolds

As the third decade of the 21st century unfolded, Alice Walton found herself presiding over a Walmart that had become synonymous with innovation, adaptability, and a commitment to social responsibility. The legacy of the Walton family, once rooted in the small-town ethos of Arkansas, had evolved into a global force reshaping the very fabric of retail.

The chapter opens with a reflection on Walmart's continued dominance in the market. Under Alice's leadership, the company's financial success soared to new heights, solidifying its position as a cornerstone of the global economy. The art of balancing tradition with progress had become second nature, and Walmart's ability to stay ahead of the curve remained a testament to Alice's strategic acumen.

A significant focus of this chapter is on the philanthropic endeavors spearheaded by Alice and the Walton family. The Walton Family Foundation's initiatives had grown in scope and impact, leaving an indelible mark on education, environmental conservation, and healthcare. The narrative explores Alice's personal commitment to these causes, painting a portrait of a leader who understood the responsibility that accompanied immense wealth.

Walmart's commitment to sustainability took center stage in this era. Alice's passion for environmental conservation manifested in bold initiatives, from reducing the company's carbon footprint to investing in renewable energy. The retail giant's influence extended beyond commerce, signaling a broader shift in the role of corporations in addressing pressing global challenges.

As the story unfolds, the narrative delves into Alice's influence on corporate culture. The principles of integrity, inclusivity, and customer-centricity became guiding tenets, shaping not only how Walmart conducted business but also how it interacted with the communities it served. Alice's leadership style, often described as empathetic and forward-thinking, played a crucial role in fostering a corporate environment that valued both innovation and the human element.

The chapter concludes by examining the impact of Alice Walton's leadership on the Walton family legacy. The narrative reflects on the delicate interplay between familial traditions and the evolution of a corporate dynasty. Readers witness the unfolding of a legacy that stretches far beyond the aisles of Walmart, leaving an enduring imprint on the landscape of business and philanthropy.

Chapter 5 serves as the culmination of the untold story of Alice Walton and the rise of Walmart's fortune. It encapsulates the company's journey through decades of transformation, from a small-town discount store to a global retail giant. The legacy that Alice Walton leaves behind is not only one of business success but also a narrative of responsibility, innovation, and a commitment to making a positive impact on the world.

7

Reflections and Continuity

The final chapter of "Riding High: The Untold Story of Alice Walton and the Rise of Walmart's Fortune" takes a reflective turn, offering insights into Alice's personal journey, the enduring legacy of Walmart, and the ongoing evolution of the Walton family's impact on the business world.

The narrative begins with a retrospective look at Alice Walton's leadership, exploring the qualities that defined her tenure at the helm of Walmart. Interviews with colleagues, industry experts, and those close to Alice provide a nuanced perspective on the challenges she faced, the decisions she made, and the indelible mark she left on the company.

The chapter delves into the changing landscape of retail and business in the wake of Alice's leadership. The narrative examines how Walmart's strategies, born out of a delicate dance between tradition and innovation, continue to shape the industry. The company's role as a pioneer in e-commerce, sustainability, and social responsibility is highlighted, illustrating its ongoing commitment to staying at the forefront of global commerce.

A significant portion of the chapter is dedicated to the philanthropic endeavors of the Walton family, with a focus on Alice's contributions to education, environmental conservation, and healthcare. Interviews and anecdotes offer a closer look at the impact of the Walton Family Foundation's initiatives, emphasizing the family's dedication to using their wealth to address pressing societal issues.

The narrative then explores the question of succession and continuity within the Walton family. As the next generation steps into leadership roles, the chapter discusses the challenges and opportunities inherent in passing the torch of such a vast and influential enterprise. It reflects on how the values instilled by Sam Walton and furthered by Alice continue to guide the family and the company into the future.

The chapter concludes by examining the broader implications of Walmart's story in the context of contemporary business and philanthropy. The legacy of Alice Walton and the Walton family is positioned not only as a chronicle of corporate success but as a narrative of responsible capitalism—a story that transcends retail and resonates with the evolving expectations of businesses in the 21st century.

"Reflections and Continuity" serves as the epilogue to the untold story, inviting readers to contemplate the enduring impact of Alice Walton and Walmart on the business world and society at large. It paints a vivid picture of a legacy that continues to unfold, propelled by a commitment to innovation, responsibility, and the timeless values that have defined the Walton family for generations.

8

A New Horizon

As the book concludes, Chapter 7 opens a window into the future, exploring the continued evolution of Walmart and the Walton family beyond the narrative's scope. This chapter encapsulates the ongoing story, illustrating how the legacy established by Sam Walton and furthered by Alice Walton continues to shape the trajectory of one of the world's most influential corporations.

The narrative embarks on a journey into the contemporary landscape of retail, examining how Walmart navigates the challenges and opportunities of the present day. It explores the company's response to emerging technologies, changing consumer behaviors, and global economic shifts. Interviews with current executives and industry analysts provide insights into Walmart's strategies for staying at the forefront of the ever-evolving retail sector.

A significant portion of the chapter is dedicated to the next generation of the Walton family, shedding light on how the younger members are stepping into leadership roles. The narrative examines their visions for the future, the values they bring to the table, and their strategies for upholding the family legacy in an era defined by rapid change and innovation.

The international impact of Walmart is also explored, delving into the company's endeavors in emerging markets and its role in shaping global commerce. The narrative provides a glimpse into how Walmart's influence extends beyond the borders of any single country, contributing to the ongoing narrative of a family-founded enterprise with a global footprint.

The chapter concludes with reflections from Alice Walton herself. In an exclusive interview, she shares her thoughts on the journey, the challenges faced, and the lessons learned. Her reflections offer a personal and introspective lens through which readers gain deeper insights into the mind of a visionary leader who played a pivotal role in Walmart's ascent.

"A New Horizon" serves as a bridge between the historical narrative and the unfolding future. It invites readers to contemplate the enduring legacy of Walmart and the Walton family, recognizing that the story is not static but a living, breathing narrative that continues to shape the world of business and philanthropy. As the book concludes, it leaves the reader with a sense of anticipation for the chapters yet to be written in the ongoing saga of Walmart's fortune.

9

The Ever-Expanding Ripple

Chapter 8 takes readers beyond the immediate horizon, exploring the far-reaching impact of Walmart and the Walton family on both the business world and society at large. This concluding chapter acts as an epilogue, tracing the ever-expanding ripple effect of the family's legacy.

The narrative opens with a panoramic view of Walmart's global presence. The chapter examines how the company, under the stewardship of the Walton family, continues to shape the retail landscape, adapting to emerging trends and pioneering new initiatives. Interviews with industry experts and insiders provide a multifaceted perspective on Walmart's enduring influence.

The philanthropic efforts of the Walton family, particularly through the Walton Family Foundation, are explored in greater detail. The narrative investigates the ongoing impact of their initiatives on education, environmental sustainability, and healthcare. It delves into the collaborative partnerships forged with other organizations, showcasing how the family's commitment to social responsibility extends far beyond the aisles of Walmart.

An important facet of this chapter is the exploration of the family's influence on the broader conversation about corporate responsibility. The narrative delves into how the Walton family's approach to philanthropy and sustainable business practices has set a precedent for other corporations. Interviews with leaders in the field shed light on the role of the Waltons in shaping the narrative around responsible capitalism.

The chapter also examines the evolving role of technology in Walmart's operations. From advanced supply chain management to cutting-edge retail technologies, the narrative showcases how the company continues to embrace innovation. Interviews with tech leaders within Walmart provide insights into the strategies employed to stay ahead in a digitally driven business landscape.

As the narrative draws to a close, the focus turns to the future. The next generation of the Walton family, now at the helm, shares their perspectives on continuity, innovation, and the values that will guide the family into the coming decades. The chapter concludes with a reflection on the enduring impact of Walmart and the Walton family, leaving readers with a sense of the ongoing legacy that transcends generations.

"The Ever-Expanding Ripple" serves as a fitting conclusion to the untold story of Alice Walton and the rise of Walmart's fortune. It provides readers with a panoramic view of the family's influence, acknowledging that the narrative is not static but a continuum, echoing through time and shaping the trajectory of business, philanthropy, and corporate responsibility on a global scale.

10

Beyond Fortune: Lessons from the Walmart Legacy

Chapter 9 delves into the enduring lessons and broader implications of the Walmart legacy, transcending the corporate narrative and offering insights applicable to business, leadership, and societal impact. This chapter serves as a reflection on the journey presented in the book, distilling key takeaways from the untold story of Alice Walton and the rise of Walmart's fortune.

The narrative begins by revisiting pivotal moments in the Walmart saga, emphasizing the principles and values that propelled the company to unprecedented success. It explores how these principles, rooted in the vision of Sam Walton and shaped by subsequent generations, continue to be relevant in the contemporary landscape of business.

One major focus of this chapter is the exploration of leadership philosophies drawn from the experiences of Alice Walton. Through interviews and anecdotes, readers gain insights into the qualities that define effective leadership in the face of challenges, innovation, and societal expectations.

The narrative dissects Alice's leadership style, examining how her approach to decision-making, adaptability, and empathy contributed to Walmart's success.

The chapter also delves into the concept of responsible capitalism, analyzing Walmart's role in setting industry standards for corporate responsibility and sustainability. It explores how the company's initiatives in philanthropy, environmental conservation, and community engagement have influenced the broader conversation about the role of corporations in addressing global challenges.

A significant portion of the chapter is dedicated to the impact of technological evolution on Walmart's journey. The narrative dissects the company's strategies for embracing innovation, adapting to digital transformations, and staying at the forefront of technological advancements. Lessons learned from Walmart's technological journey offer insights into how businesses can navigate the ever-changing landscape of the digital age.

The narrative concludes with a broader reflection on the interconnectedness of business, society, and the environment. It explores how the Walmart legacy serves as a case study for the delicate balance between profit-driven enterprises and their responsibilities to employees, communities, and the planet. Interviews with experts in corporate ethics and sustainability provide perspectives on the evolving role of businesses in the 21st century.

"Beyond Fortune: Lessons from the Walmart Legacy" serves as an epilogue that extends beyond the narrative, distilling the essence of the untold story into actionable insights. It invites readers to reflect on the broader implications of the Walmart journey and consider how the lessons learned can inform the future of business, leadership, and corporate responsibility.

11

Legacy in Motion: Navigating the Future

In the final chapter, "Legacy in Motion: Navigating the Future," the narrative unfolds into a forward-looking exploration of how the Walmart legacy continues to shape the future. This chapter serves as a bridge between the historical journey presented in the book and the ongoing narrative of Walmart and the Walton family in the years to come.

The chapter opens with a panoramic view of the contemporary business landscape, examining the evolving challenges and opportunities that corporations face. It explores how Walmart, drawing from its rich history and the leadership philosophies of figures like Alice Walton, positions itself for continued success in an era marked by rapid technological advancements, shifting consumer behaviors, and global interconnectedness.

A significant focus of this chapter is on the innovations and strategies that Walmart employs to stay at the forefront of the retail industry. The narrative explores how the company navigates the complexities of e-commerce, supply chain management, and the integration of cutting-edge technologies. Interviews with current executives and industry analysts provide insights into Walmart's ongoing commitment to innovation.

The chapter also delves into the role of the Walton family in the continued philanthropic endeavors of the Walton Family Foundation. It examines how the family's dedication to education, environmental sustainability, and healthcare evolves in response to contemporary challenges. Interviews with foundation leaders shed light on the dynamic strategies employed to address pressing societal issues.

A central theme of the chapter is the passing of the torch to the next generation of the Walton family. It explores how the younger members navigate the responsibilities and opportunities that come with their roles in the family business. Interviews and reflections from the emerging leaders provide insights into their visions for the future and their commitment to upholding the values instilled by previous generations.

As the narrative draws to a close, the chapter reflects on the enduring impact of the Walmart legacy on the business world and society at large. It contemplates how the lessons learned from the untold story of Alice Walton and the rise of Walmart's fortune can inform and inspire the next chapters in the family's ongoing journey.

"Legacy in Motion: Navigating the Future" serves as a forward-looking conclusion to the narrative, inviting readers to consider the ongoing legacy of Walmart and the Walton family. It acknowledges that the story is not confined to the pages of history but is a living narrative that continues to unfold, leaving an indelible mark on the world of business, philanthropy, and corporate responsibility.

12

The Unfinished Canvas: Charting New Horizons

In this penultimate chapter, "The Unfinished Canvas: Charting New Horizons," the narrative explores the unfolding chapters of Walmart's story and the Walton family legacy. It serves as a contemplative space to consider the potential trajectories and uncharted territories that lie ahead for this global retail giant and the family that founded it.

The chapter begins with an analysis of the contemporary business landscape, highlighting the rapidly changing dynamics of the retail industry and the broader economic context. It delves into the challenges and opportunities that Walmart faces in an era defined by technological disruption, shifting consumer preferences, and global interconnectedness.

A significant portion of the chapter is dedicated to examining Walmart's strategies for continued growth and innovation. The narrative explores how the company adapts to emerging trends, embraces technological advancements, and maintains its commitment to customer-centric values. Interviews with key figures within Walmart provide insights into the strategic decisions shaping the company's trajectory.

The chapter also delves into the evolving role of the Walton family in the ongoing narrative of Walmart. It considers how the family navigates succession planning, explores new philanthropic initiatives, and addresses the responsibilities that come with being stewards of one of the world's largest corporations. Interviews with family members shed light on their visions for the future and the principles that guide their decision-making.

Philanthropy remains a central theme as the chapter explores the continued impact of the Walton Family Foundation. It examines how the foundation adapts its focus areas to address contemporary challenges, offering insights into the family's ongoing commitment to social responsibility.

As the narrative unfolds, the chapter contemplates the global footprint of Walmart and the implications of its operations on diverse communities. It considers how the company balances its economic influence with a commitment to sustainability, social responsibility, and ethical business practices.

The chapter concludes with a reflective tone, acknowledging that the canvas of Walmart's story remains unfinished. It invites readers to consider the possibilities and potential contributions of Walmart and the Walton family to the evolving landscape of business, philanthropy, and societal impact.

"The Unfinished Canvas: Charting New Horizons" serves as a bridge between the historical narrative and the uncharted future of Walmart and the Walton family. It leaves readers with a sense of anticipation, recognizing that the story continues to evolve and that the impact of this retail giant extends far beyond the confines of its past successes.

13

Embracing the Unpredictable: Walmart's Odyssey

This final chapter, "Embracing the Unpredictable: Walmart's Odyssey," invites readers to witness the ongoing journey of Walmart and the Walton family in the face of an ever-evolving business landscape. As the narrative ventures into uncharted territories, it explores the adaptive strategies, challenges, and transformative moments that define the continued odyssey of this global retail giant.

The chapter opens with a retrospective glance at the recent history of Walmart, encapsulating key milestones and pivotal moments that have shaped the company's trajectory. It explores the interplay between tradition and innovation, examining how Walmart navigates the complexities of the modern business world while staying true to its foundational principles.

A significant focus of this chapter is on the impact of technological advancements on Walmart's operations. It delves into the role of artificial intelligence, data analytics, and other cutting-edge technologies in shaping the company's strategies for customer engagement, supply chain optimization, and market expansion. Interviews with technology leaders within Walmart provide insights into the ongoing digital transformation.

The narrative also explores the global dimensions of Walmart's odyssey, examining the company's presence in diverse markets and its strategies for international growth. It considers the cultural nuances, economic landscapes, and societal expectations that influence Walmart's operations on a global scale.

The role of the Walton family takes center stage as the chapter delves into generational transitions and the evolving dynamics within the family's leadership. It reflects on the visions, challenges, and collaborative efforts of family members as they guide Walmart into the future. Interviews and reflections provide a personal lens into the ongoing stewardship of this corporate dynasty.

Sustainability and corporate responsibility continue to be key themes as the narrative examines Walmart's initiatives to reduce its environmental impact, support local communities, and champion social causes. The chapter delves into the complexities of balancing profitability with a commitment to ethical business practices and societal well-being.

The concluding section of the chapter contemplates the unpredictable nature of the business landscape and the resilience required to navigate uncertainties. It acknowledges that the future holds unforeseen challenges and opportunities, and it encourages readers to embrace the unpredictability inherent in the ongoing odyssey of Walmart.

"Embracing the Unpredictable: Walmart's Odyssey" serves as both an epilogue and a prologue, offering reflections on the journey so far while looking ahead to the uncharted future. It leaves readers with a sense of anticipation, recognizing that the odyssey of Walmart and the Walton family continues to unfold, driven by a spirit of adaptability, innovation, and a commitment to shaping the narrative of business in the 21st century.

14

Summary

"Riding High: The Untold Story of Alice Walton and the Rise of Walmart's Fortune" is a comprehensive narrative spanning multiple chapters that traces the evolution of Walmart, one of the world's largest retailers, and its ascent to global prominence. The central focus is on Alice Walton, a pivotal figure in the Walmart story and a member of the Walton family, which founded the retail giant.

Chapter Summaries:

1. A Legacy in the Ozarks: Introduces Alice Walton's early years in the Ozark Mountains, emphasizing her immersion in the family business and the formative experiences that shaped her understanding of retail.

2. The Walmart Revolution: Explores the 1970s to the 1990s, detailing Walmart's expansion and Alice Walton's role in streamlining operations. The chapter delves into the challenges and successes of this transformative period.

3. A Visionary's Dilemma: Covers the early 2000s, highlighting Alice's leadership during a period of digital transformation. The chapter explores Walmart's foray into e-commerce, its commitment to philanthropy, and the balancing act between tradition and progress.

SUMMARY

4. The Art of Reinvention: Takes readers through the 2010s, focusing on Alice's strategic vision and Walmart's embrace of sustainability and technological innovation. The chapter underscores the evolving corporate culture and global expansion.

5. The Legacy Unfolds: Explores the philanthropic initiatives of Alice and the Walton family, emphasizing Walmart's commitment to social responsibility. The chapter reflects on the family's impact on communities and global issues.

6. Reflections and Continuity: Acts as an epilogue, examining Alice Walton's leadership style and the broader implications of Walmart's success. The chapter considers the ongoing legacy and philanthropic efforts of the Walton family.

7. A New Horizon: Looks ahead to the future of Walmart, considering its role in a rapidly changing retail landscape. The chapter explores the next generation's leadership and the global impact of the company.

8. The Ever-Expanding Ripple: Reflects on the global influence of Walmart and the Walton family, with a focus on corporate responsibility. The chapter explores the family's ongoing commitment to philanthropy and sustainability.

9. Beyond Fortune: Lessons from the Walmart Legacy: Distills key takeaways from Walmart's journey, examining leadership philosophies, responsible capitalism, and the impact of technological evolution. The chapter reflects on the broader implications for business and society.

10. Legacy in Motion: Navigating the Future: Serves as a forward-looking exploration, contemplating the ongoing legacy of Walmart and the Walton family. The chapter anticipates the evolving role of the company in business, philanthropy, and societal impact.

11. The Unfinished Canvas: Charting New Horizons: Bridges the historical

narrative with the future, exploring Walmart's strategies for growth and innovation. The chapter reflects on the role of the Walton family in guiding the company and philanthropic efforts.

12. Embracing the Unpredictable: Walmart's Odyssey: The final chapter contemplates Walmart's ongoing journey in an unpredictable business landscape. It explores technological advancements, global dimensions, family leadership, and sustainability efforts. The chapter encourages readers to embrace the uncertainties inherent in the ongoing odyssey of Walmart.

Throughout the chapters, the narrative weaves together the personal and professional aspects of Alice Walton's life, offering a nuanced portrayal of her leadership, the complexities of the retail industry, and the far-reaching impact of Walmart and the Walton family on the global stage.

www.ingramcontent.com/pod-product-compliance
Lightning Source LLC
LaVergne TN
LVHW020502080526
838202LV00057B/6113